DUPUIS

Drip c112

Cool Melons— Turn to Frogs!

The Life and Poems of Issa

Story and Haiku Translations
by Matthew Gollub

Illustrations by Kazuko G. Stone

Calligraphy by Keiko Smith

Lee & Low Books, Inc. • New York

LEE & LOW BOOKS, Inc., 95 Madison Avenue,
New York, NY 10016

Printed in Hong Kong by South China Printing Co. (1988) Ltd.

Book design by Tania Garcia
Book production by The Kids at Our House

The text is set in 15 pt. Centaur
The illustrations are rendered in watercolor and colored pencil. The
image of Kashiwabara, Issa's village, that appears on this page was
inspired by the photographs of Totaro Koshi.

10 9 8 7 6 5 4 3 2
First Edition

Library of Congress Cataloging-in-Publication Data
Gollub, Matthew
  Cool melons—turn to frogs!: the life and poems of Issa/
by Matthew Gollub; illustrated by Kazuko Stone.—1st ed.
    p.   cm.
  Summary: A biography and introduction to the work
of the Japanese haiku poet whose love for nature
finds expression in the more than thirty poems included
in this book.
  ISBN 1-880000-71-7
  1. Kobayashi, Issa 1763–1827—xJuvenile literature. 2. Poets,
Japanese—Edo period, 1600–1868—Biography—Juvenile literature.
[1. Kobayashi, Issa, 1763-1827. 2. Poets, Japanese. 3. Haiku.]
I. Stone, Kazuko G., ill. II. Title.
PL797.2.Z5G65 1998
895.6'134—dc21   98-13087
                                                       CIP AC

To Kalane and Jacob — M.G.
For Robert, who loves Japan — K.G.S.

Issa was born long ago in a small mountain village in Japan. In the spring, plum blossoms washed through the air, and Issa heard farmers sing as they planted rice. Insect cries lasted through summer, and warm rains pattered on his home's thatched roof.

By autumn, Issa was old enough to crawl outside. He watched his father cut the heavy rice stalks. His mother threshed and stored the grain. During the long snowy winter, he kept warm near the fireplace. Then when spring returned, he would rush outside where the sounds of laughing children would melt away the snow.

In the mountains, these four seasons changed a little each day and filled Issa's world with discoveries.

Plum tree in bloom —

a cat's silhouette

upon the paper screen.

梅咲くや しきゃびに猫の 影法師

霞のむ つまんでみなる わらべ哉

A child intent

on plucking jewels

of dew in the morning grass.

A kitten

stamps on falling leaves,

holds them to the ground.

猫の子が　ちよいと押へる　おち葉哉

Mouth-watering snowflakes fall,

lightly, lightly,

heaven's snack.

うまそうな　雪がふうはりふはり哉

When Issa was three, his mother passed away. His grandmother took care of him every day. But often Issa played alone in the woods. He watched for birds and listened for insects. And for the rest of his life, he considered them his friends.

Motherless sparrow,

come play

with me.

寝るてふに かつておぶさる 脈がしら

Rest here

sleepy butterfly,

I'll lend you my lap.

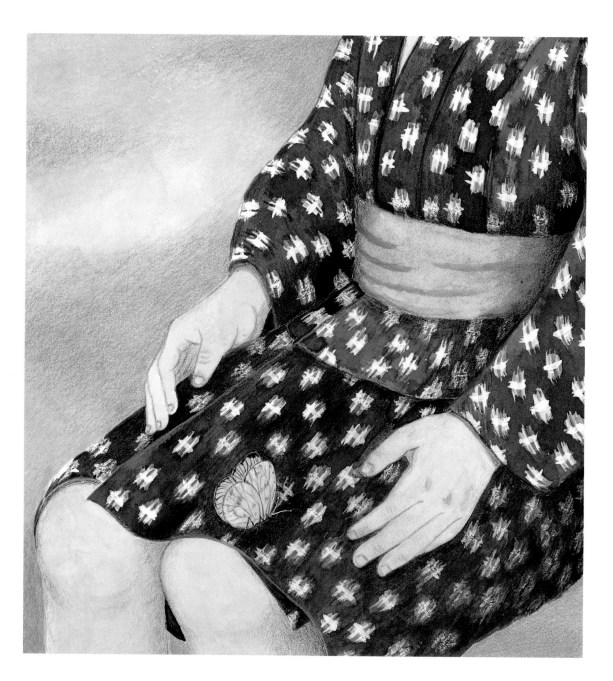

Locusts riding piggy-back,

hopping

over a stream.

みぞりを おぶさつてとぶ いなご哉

云てぶんの　あるつらつきや　引がへる

By the time Issa was seven, his father had remarried, and it was time for Issa to go to the village school. Issa liked to study, but his stepmother felt that he should help his father work in the fields instead. In the end, she denied Issa even a candle by which to read his lessons at night.

Soon Issa's stepmother gave birth to a son. She often made Issa look after the baby, then scolded Issa when the baby cried. This made Issa both angry and sad. His schoolmaster noticed that he was unhappy and encouraged Issa to write haiku. "With haiku," he said, "you can show what you are feeling inside."

A silent toad—

the face of one

bursting with much to say.

Oni-gawara,

a face so fierce

he'd snap at the wintry moon.

寒月や 啗ひつきそうな 鬼瓦

Issa's father took pride in his son's poems, and that made Issa's stepmother jealous. "What a lazy boy you are, writing useless verse!" she sneered. "Why don't you do some real work rather than live off your father's sweat?"

"But Father told me to study," protested Issa. "And all this shouting is making my brother cry!"

A bamboo stick—

a stepchild

scratches characters in the dirt.

Issa and his stepmother eventually quarreled so much that his father, in desperation, decided to send his son away. When Issa was fourteen, he and his father left the house. Issa's father walked with him as far as a mountain road to the capital. "Son, you have a gift, but it cannot grow in this soil. Go now, and promise me I'll see your healthy face again."

Issa stood silently, then bowed his farewell.

Lilies blooming

thick and fast,

a skylark's lonesome cry.

On the road, Issa joined travelers headed for Edo, the capital of Japan.

In Edo, which is now called Tokyo, he found a bustling city brimming with fancy homes and shops. People spoke quickly, and their hurried manner confused him. At times, Issa found work as a stable boy or servant. But other times, he went hungry and had no place to sleep. Still, he noticed little things that most people were too busy to see.

Sparrow chicks—

Look out! Look out!

Make way for Mr. Horse.

A newborn butterfly,

a dog's dish—a place

to sleep through the night!

初蝶の 一夜寝にけり 犬の椀

There!

Atop the eggplant horse

a cricket hitches a ride.

蛉の

ふいと乗りけり

茄子馬

Climb Mount Fuji,

Snail, but slowly,

slowly!

For years, Issa longed to visit his father. But he knew that he and his stepmother would quarrel. So instead of saving his pennies to go home, he made up his mind to buy ink and brushes. Then as a young man, he asked a master poet for training.

"I have no money to pay you, but I can do chores," Issa offered.

Between dusting and sweeping the master's classrooms, Issa kept notes of all that he learned. Soon Issa's poems were being published in books. And before long, the master asked him to run the academy himself!

New Year's—

even the Buddha wears

a bright red hood for luck.

The rare beauty

of green bamboo shoots

sprouting here and there.

うしや やうけのの つ〜〜と

秋の夜や旅の男の針仕事

In the end, Issa didn't care for teaching formal classes. Students complained that his casual manner was not befitting of a haiku master. Meanwhile, all Issa really wanted was to continue writing and see more of the world. So in the spring of his thirtieth year, Issa set out traveling in the tradition of haiku poets. He shaved his head, wore a priestly robe and carried a pilgrim's staff.

Although he was not tall, he had a sturdy build, and his large hands and feet helped him climb steep paths. Often he slept in Buddhist temples where monks gave him food and shelter for the night. In return, Issa helped the monks with their poems, and he found pleasure in even the simple moments of moving from place to place.

Needlework —

a traveling man's

comfort this autumn night.

Asleep on the ocean —

a folding fan

shades me from the moon.

海
の
月

扇
か
ぶ
っ
て

寝
た
り
け
り

禍の神 やとらせ冷ふ ぼたん哉

For seven years, Issa journeyed around Japan by foot. And his travels put him in closer contact with nature than ever before.

A giant peony,

rich and full,

surely the God of Wealth dwells within.

Mother, father and child monkey,

also take soothing baths —

spring breeze.

春風に　猿もおや子の　湯治哉

遠山が

目にうつる

とんぼ哉

A distant mountain

shimmers in the

dragonfly's eye.

A withered tree

blooms once again—

butterflies holding fast.

べったりと
蝶の咲たる
枯木哉

The new year's first dream —

I see my village

and wake to a chilly tear.

初夢に古郷をみて涙哉

When Issa at last returned to his village, his father had fallen gravely ill. "Son," his father gasped, "forgive me for sending you away while you were so young."

Tears streamed down Issa's face. "But I must beg your forgiveness, Father. I left you to toil in the fields all these years!"

Issa stayed by his father's bedside and nursed him during his final months. Then his father made one request. "Son, you may not get along with my wife. But the house and land, though meager, are part yours. Promise me you'll settle here and start a family of your own."

For years, Issa's stepfamily refused to share the old farm-house. The two sides finally built a wall down the middle of the house. Only then, without speaking to each other, could they live side by side.

When Issa was fifty-one, he married a young woman from the village. Her name was Kiku, which means "chrysanthemum," but Issa likened her to a dove.

Spring rain—

The dove tells the owl

to fix his worried face.

Soon Kiku gave birth to Sato, a baby girl who made Issa's heart sing with joy.

Crawl! Laugh! Just like that.

You're two years old

this morning.

Baby firefly—

Do my hand's wrinkles

make it hard to walk?

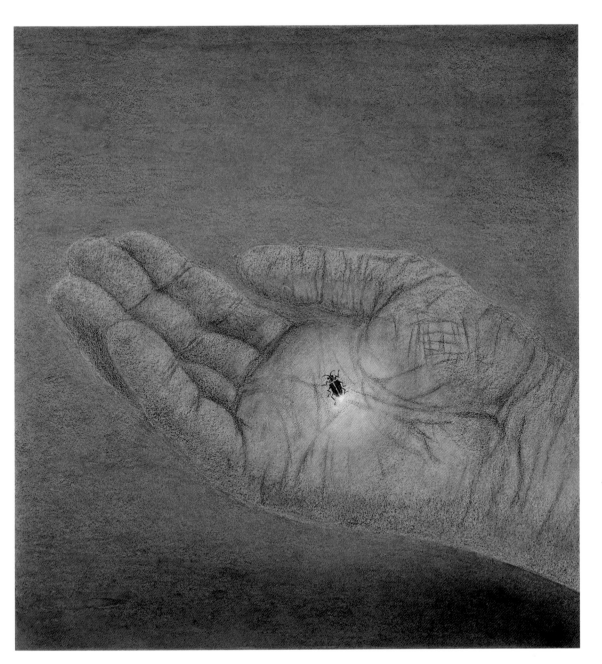

手の皺が　歩み悪いか　初螢

露
の
世
の
つ
ゆ
の
せ
な
が
ら
さ
り
な
が
ら

But Sato died of smallpox after she turned two. In his grief, Issa compared her to a dewdrop world—precious yet fleeting like the dewdrops of spring.

A dewdrop world,

so fresh, so precious,

like morning dew slips away.

Issa continued to face much sorrow. He lost one child after another at a time when only the healthiest people survived. Then he lost his wife, Kiku, as well.

Still, he found solace in writing haiku. And, despite the sadness that shadowed his life, he brought cheer to his many friends and inspiration to students. One night, during a party his students gave him, Issa composed a hundred haiku!

In this world

even among insects,

some sing well, some don't.

やれ打つな 塊が手をすり 足をする

Issa never lost his affection for small creatures—or for almost anything he found along his path.

Please, don't swat!

the housefly begs,

rubbing its hands and feet.

Once when he saw watermelons left outside to chill, he felt sorry that someone would soon eat them up. If only, he wished, they could hop away, then people would leave them alone!

Cool melons—

turn to frogs!

If people should come near.

Issa died in his snowy village at the age of sixty-four. In all, he wrote over 20,000 haiku. He is known to people of all ages in Japan, and now he is known to you.

じっと雪をくらすや牧の駒

A motionless horse,

at peace in the field,

in the quietly falling snow.

O wild goose,

how young were you

when you set out alone?

雁よ「いくつのとしから 旅をした

AUTHOR'S NOTE

Kazuko and I selected these poems both for their inherent charm and for the light they shed on Issa's life. Issa did not necessarily write each haiku in the same chronology described in the book. Still, the poems are rooted in his experience. Like seeds lying dormant beneath the earth, sentiments often wait years to surface. By freely interspersing Issa's haiku with the major, formative events of his life, we sought to provide an insightful way for readers to appreciate his work.

"Brother Issa" (1763–1827): *Issa's given name at birth was Kobayashi Yataro. Although he was commonly known as Issa (pronounced EE-sa), the entire name that he later adopted was "Haikaiji Nyudo Issa-bo," or "Brother Issa, Lay Priest of the Temple of Poetry."*

Kazuko began the research for *Cool Melons* by reading more than 2,500 of Issa's poems. I translated her favorites into English and studied still others that I'd found in English and Japanese haiku collections. Later, Kazuko journeyed to Issa's village, Kashiwabara, which is a four-hour train ride from her native Tokyo. The farmhouse, which caused so much trouble during his life, had burned to the ground in Issa's old age. Issa lived his last years in a structure built for storing grain. Today that structure and Issa's personal items, including his calligraphy brushes and original manuscripts, are preserved as he left them.

Each poem featured in this book is rendered in Japanese in the outer page margins. The style of calligraphy uses cursive, rather than square, letters to better suggest the spontaneity of their creation. Keiko prepared the calligraphy using traditional materials: charcoal, water, paper, and brush. Here's how Issa's name looks in Japanese written in square letters by Keiko with a brush:

Some readers may appreciate background notes on the following poems that appear in this book. Japanese transliterations are provided to give an idea of what the poems sound like in the original Japanese. Vowels in Japanese are pronounced like those of Spanish: "a" as *ah*, "e" as *eh*, "i" as *ee*, "o" as *oh*, and "u" as *oo*. Japanese words do not have stress accents (as in EN-glish), so while reading the Japanese try to give equal emphasis to all syllables.

Motherless sparrow, / come play / with me.
Ware-to-kite asobe-ya-oya-no nai-suzume
Issa wrote this poem when he was just six years old.

Oni-gawara, / a face so fierce / he'd snap at the wintry moon.
Kan-getsu-ya kui-tsuki-soh-na oni-gawara
An *oni-gawara* is a guardian perched on the ridge of a temple's roof. In order to scare away goblins and ghosts, it's his job to look downright mean.

There! / Atop the eggplant horse / a cricket hitches a ride.
Koh-rogi-no fuito-norikeri nasubi-uma
During *O-bon*, Japan's summer festival to honor the dead, children sometimes place "horses" on household altars, using eggplants or cucumbers for the horses' bodies and toothpicks for their legs. Ancestral spirits then can ride the horses home for a visit.

Crawl! Laugh! Just like that. / You're two years old / this morning.
Hae-wara-e futatsu-ni-naruzo kesa-kara-wa
Although Issa wrote "you're two years old," to our way of thinking, his daughter was less than one. Traditionally, in Japan people were considered a year old at birth. And everyone turned a year older on New Year's day, regardless of when they were actually born.

ABOUT THE TRANSLATIONS

In Japanese, a haiku must contain exactly seventeen syllables. The poems are written on three different lines, the first line containing five syllables, the second line seven, and the third line five. But since Japanese words generally have more syllables than English (e.g., "snail" in English contains just one syllable, while the Japanese word, *ka-ta-tsu-mu-ri*, contains five), most haiku require fewer syllables in translation. Rather than embellish the poems with extra syllables to make seventeen, I tried to interpret the haiku succinctly, and otherwise not complicate their simplicity and charm.

ABOUT HAIKU

Even before the time of Issa, Japanese poets had written haiku for centuries. Traditional haiku describe a single moment in nature, something that the poet observes or discovers. As such, a haiku can refresh or enlighten us by calling to mind life's passing details.

A haiku, because of its brevity, resembles a quick line sketch. It's up to the reader to imagine the details and to make the picture complete. In a sense, we can think of a haiku as a telegraph; for example: "Should arrive Tuesday, supper time." From this short message, we can infer that, weather permitting, the sender will arrive early on Tuesday evening, and that after the long, tiresome journey she would appreciate a good meal.

Often, haiku describe two events side by side, such as: "Plum tree in bloom —/a cat's silhouette/upon the paper screen." Does the silhouette of the plum tree also appear on the paper screen? Does the plum tree in bloom suggest the warmth of a spring day? Again, it's up to the reader to imagine how or if the two things are related.

Almost all traditional haiku convey a sense of season. But rather than name the season outright, most haiku rely on a *kigo* — a word or phrase to suggest the season indirectly. For example, "blossom" is a *kigo* for spring; "New Year's" suggests winter; "firefly" implies summer; and "painted leaves" tells us that the season is fall. Can you figure out the season suggested by each poem in this book?

Finally, haiku tend to be simple and understated, so there's never one "correct" way to interpret them. The idea is to ponder each poem's imagery and to discover and enjoy how the poem makes you feel.

By now, haiku have touched people in more countries than the Japanese masters of old may have dreamed. Poets around the world write haiku in their own languages. Haiku societies have sprouted up like bamboo shoots, and many new forms of haiku have evolved, with themes of humor, satire, romance, and modern life, replacing the traditional focus on nature. Whether you write haiku in the traditional or modern style, there's no better time than now to listen and observe, and to capture one meaningful moment in time. —M.G.